BRAVE THE BIOME

DESERT SURVIVAL GUIDE

SARAH EASON

CRABTREE
PUBLISHING COMPANY
WWW.CRABTREEBOOKS.COM

BRAVE THE BIOME

Author: Sarah Eason

Editors: Jennifer Sanderson and Ellen Rodger

Proofreader and indexer: Tracey Kelly

Proofreader: Petrice Custance

Editorial director: Kathy Middleton

Design: Jessica Moon

Cover design: Tammy McGarr

Photo research: Rachel Blount

Production coordinator and Prepress technician: Tammy McGarr

Print coordinator: Katherine Berti

Consultant: David Hawksett

Produced for Crabtree Publishing by Calcium

Photo Credits:
t=Top, c=Center, b=Bottom, l= Left, r=Right

Inside: Jessica Moon: pp. 17b, 29t; Shutterstock: Alina E: pp. 30-31; ArtMari: p. 13b; Michal Balada: p. 10b; Ruth Black: p. 4b; Steve Bruckmann: pp. 20-21; Denis Burdin: pp. 4-5; Chris971: p. 7b; Nik Coli: pp. 22-23; John Copland: p. 19t; Kleber Cordeiro: p. 14l; Dean Drobot: p. 22b; EcoPrint: p. 12; Filip Fuxa: pp. 26-27; Bernadette Heath: p. 13r; JulezHohlfeld: pp. 10-11; LapailrKrapai: pp. 18-19; Jon Manjeot: pp. 14-15; Maridav: p. 9; Marques: pp. 6-7; MAV Drone: p. 24t; Micha17: pp. 12-13; Patsy Michaud: p. 21; Mureu: p. 23b; Nejron Photo: p. 11r; Nikiteev_konstantin: pp. 6b, 11b; Nomadkate: pp. 28-29b; Novak.elcic: p. 26; Charles T. Peden: p. 5t; Peek Creative Collective: p. 32; Pred.Pop: pp. 16-17; Ondrej Prosicky: p. 17t; Joshua Resnick: pp. 24-25; Padma Sanjaya: p. 19b; Dmitry Shanchuk: p. 24b; John D Sirlin: pp. 6-7c; Sirtravelalot: pp. 8-9; Kathryn Weiss: p. 23t; Hamdan Yoshida: pp. 28-29bg.

Cover: expatpostcards: cover br; All other images from Shutterstock

Library and Archives Canada Cataloguing in Publication

Title: Desert survival guide / Sarah Eason.
Names: Eason, Sarah, author.
Description: Series statement: Brave the biome | Includes index.
Identifiers: Canadiana (print) 20200285572 | Canadiana (ebook) 20200285580 | ISBN 9780778781325 (softcover) | ISBN 9780778781264 (hardcover) | ISBN 9781427125729 (HTML)
Subjects: LCSH: Desert survival—Juvenile literature. | LCSH: Survival—Juvenile literature. | LCSH: Deserts—Juvenile literature.
Classification: LCC GV200.5 .E27 2021 | DDC j613.6/909154—dc23

Library of Congress Cataloging-in-Publication Data

Names: Eason, Sarah, author.
Title: Desert survival guide / Sarah Eason.
Description: New York : Crabtree Publishing Company, [2021] | Series: Brave the biome | Includes index.
Identifiers: LCCN 2020029904 (print) | LCCN 2020029905 (ebook) | ISBN 9780778781264 (hardcover) | ISBN 9780778781325 (paperback) | ISBN 9781427125729 (ebook)
Subjects: LCSH: Desert survival--Juvenile literature.
Classification: LCC GV200.5 .E25 2021 (print) | LCC GV200.5 (ebook) | DDC 613.6/9--dc23
LC record available at https://lccn.loc.gov/2020029904
LC ebook record available at https://lccn.loc.gov/2020029905

Crabtree Publishing Company

www.crabtreebooks.com 1-800-387-7650

Printed in the U.S.A./092020/CG20200810

Published in Canada
Crabtree Publishing
616 Welland Ave.
St. Catharines, Ontario
L2M 5V6

Published in the United States
Crabtree Publishing
347 Fifth Ave.
Suite 1402-145
New York, NY 10016

Published in the United Kingdom
Crabtree Publishing
Maritime House
Basin Road North, Hove
BN41 1WR

Published in Australia
Crabtree Publishing
3 Charles Street
Coburg North
VIC, 3058

CONTENTS

A desert is any place that gets fewer than 10 inches (25 cm) of precipitation a year. Precipitation is water that reaches the ground, such as rain, snow, or hail. There are four types of desert: hot and dry, cold winter, coastal, and polar. This book looks mainly at survival in hot and dry deserts. These deserts can reach scorching temperatures during the day and be freezing cold at night. Animals and plants that live there have **adapted** to the harsh conditions. For humans who find themselves stranded in a desert, survival is not easy. To survive, they must rely on skills that can make the difference between life and death.

SURVIVING IN SANDY DESERTS

The Sahara in North Africa is the biggest sandy desert in the world. This hot and dry desert is flat and stony but also has towering sand **dunes**. Very few plants grow there. The camels that live there have adapted to the sandy environment in many ways. They have large, flat feet that help keep them from sinking into the soft sand. Their long eyelashes protect their eyes in **sandstorms**. People who travel through sandy deserts must dress and equip themselves to be protected from the harsh sun and sandstorms.

The **nomadic** people who live in the Sahara wear head coverings for protection from the cold, Sun, and wind.

SURVIVING ROCKY DESERTS

The Sonoran Desert is a hot, dry, and rocky desert that stretches along the southwestern coast of the United States. The ground there is stony. Cactus plants have adapted to the hot, dry weather by growing spines that store water. One survival skill that can be used by people who are stranded in a rocky desert is to drink water stored in the branches of the cactus plant.

saguaro cactus, Sonoran Desert

LOOK FOR ...

Look for the "How to Survive" and "Be Prepared" features in this book. These list many of the techniques that people have used to survive in deserts.

PREPARE TO SURVIVE

Before going into the desert, there are some safety rules to follow. Anyone going to the desert should always travel in a group with a guide. The guide should be someone who knows the area and its dangers. Hikers should always plan their route and give that information to someone not going with them. It is a good idea for this person to have a copy of the route, clearly drawn on an up-to-date map. They should also know when the group will return and alert rescue services if the hikers do not arrive on time.

sandstorm, Sonoran Desert

STAY WITH THE GROUP

Once the group has set off, the route should never be changed unless it is absolutely necessary. Individuals should never leave the group to explore by themselves. A lone explorer can find themselves in dangerous situations. They could encounter sudden sand or rainstorms that set them off course. If they have an accident, there will be no one to help.

HOW TO PACK FOR THE DESERT

When packing for the desert, a survival kit is very important. This can be a bag that contains emergency essentials such as:

- knife
- mirror for signaling for help
- water **purifying** tablets
- compass
- plastic bag
- whistle
- basic first aid items
- something to light a fire
- cream for sunburn

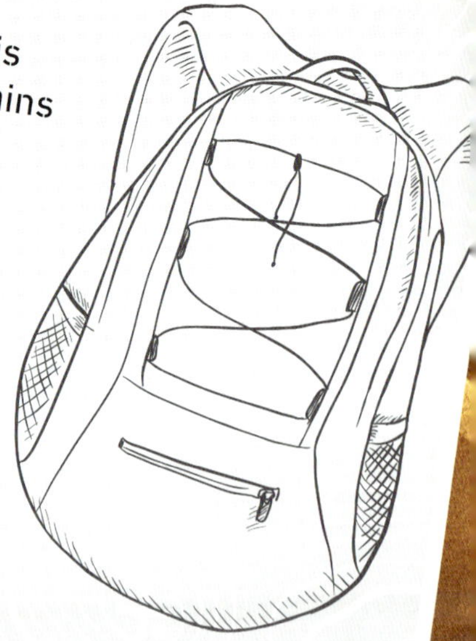

DO NOT DEHYDRATE

The biggest danger in the desert is **dehydration**. Symptoms of dehydration include feeling very thirsty, a dry mouth, feeling tired and dizzy, and having headaches. Resting during the day and moving around at night when it is cooler can help prevent dehydration. If someone becomes dehydrated, lying down under some shade, raised off the hot ground if possible, can help them. Their clothing should be loosened, and a cool compress, such as a handkerchief or material soaked in water, can be used on their head and neck to cool them down. It is important to keep still and cool, and take regular sips of water.

Drinking water is essential for desert explorers. Experts usually plan for 1 gallon (3.8 l) of water per person, per day. This does not include water needed for cooking.

SURVIVAL STORY

STORM OF NEEDLES: MAURO PROSPERI

In 1994, Mauro Prosperi was competing in Marathon des Sables in the Sahara Desert when he was hit by a sandstorm. The race is so dangerous that competitors sign a form to say where they would like their body to be sent in case they die. The event attracts more than 1,000 entrants today, but in 1994, only a few runners were up to the challenge.

DISASTER STRIKES

The six-day race began well for Mauro. He had trained hard and was ready. But on the fourth day, disaster struck. Mauro was running alone in sand dunes when suddenly he found himself in the middle of a sandstorm. In the worst storms, strong winds can lift the sand 10 to 50 feet (3 to 15 m) into the air and travel at speeds of 25 miles per hour (40 km/h). Mauro was surrounded by a blinding wall of sand. He could not see or breathe. The sharp particles of sand felt like needles whipping his face.

TOTALLY LOST

Mauro covered his head and face with his scarf to keep the sand from cutting him and going into his eyes, ears, nose, and mouth. He crouched down in a sheltered spot to wait for the storm to pass. When the storm died down, Mauro realized it had changed the way the landscape looked. He had no idea which way to go. Luckily, Mauro knew a little about desert survival. He walked slowly when it was cool in the early morning and evening, and rested during the day. He wore a cap and a wool hat to keep his temperature **stable**.

On the second day, Mauro heard a helicopter. He fired a **flare**, but the pilot did not see it. When Mauro reached a building used by nomads, he decided to stay there until rescuers came for him.

RESCUE

On the third day of being lost, Mauro heard a plane engine, so he quickly made a fire by burning his rucksack and anything else he had to create smoke. However, another sandstorm hit, and the plane flew past. Mauro decided to head for the clouds he could see on the horizon at dawn, hoping that they would lead him to safety. After several more days, he came across dried goat droppings and followed them. They led to a group of Tuareg nomads who gave him goat's milk and took him to the nearest village. He was dehydrated, close to starvation, and his eyes and liver were damaged—but he had survived.

Like Mauro, athletes must train specifically for desert running, which tests the body far more than running in cooler conditions. Runners try to train in hot desertlike environments, so that they are used to the heat and the type of land.

DRESS FOR THE DESERT

The scorching desert Sun can be dangerous. Sunburn can cause the skin to turn red and become blistered and sore. Eventually, the skin peels off. Sunstroke causes dizziness, headaches, vomiting, and cramps. Desert hikers should wear hats, sunglasses, long-sleeved shirts, and long pants to stay safe.

COPY THE DESERT PEOPLE

The Sun causes people to sweat more as the body tries to keep cool. This means that the body loses water, which can cause dehydration. Desert peoples, such as the Bedouin of North Africa's Sahara Desert, wear loose clothing to trap sweat against the skin, reducing water loss. Bedouin men wear a long dress-like garment called a thoab, and the women wear a madraga. These loose garments also help keep them cool.

During the day, the Bedouin wear a scarf around their head. It is called a shemagh. A shemagh is made by folding a square scarf in half to form a triangle. The scarf goes over the head, with one side hanging down longer than the other. The short length is wrapped around the neck to the back of the head. The long end is wrapped across the chin and nose, then around the back of the head. The two ends are knotted together at the back to keep the scarf in place.

DRESS TO SURVIVE

Wearing long-sleeved tops and loose pants, rather than short-sleeved T-shirts and shorts, is a good idea for desert explorers. A wide-brimmed hat is much better than a baseball cap. At night, the temperature in the desert can drop, so a warm jacket and a wool hat are also essential. Sturdy hiking boots or shoes with thick soles protect the feet against cactus spines, sharp rocks, and the heat of the sand. It is important for shoes to have a liner between the main body and the tongue of the shoe. This will keep sand, gravel, or small stones from getting into the shoes.

Even if hikers are not camping overnight, they should be prepared and carry extra warm clothes in their backpacks.

BE PREPARED

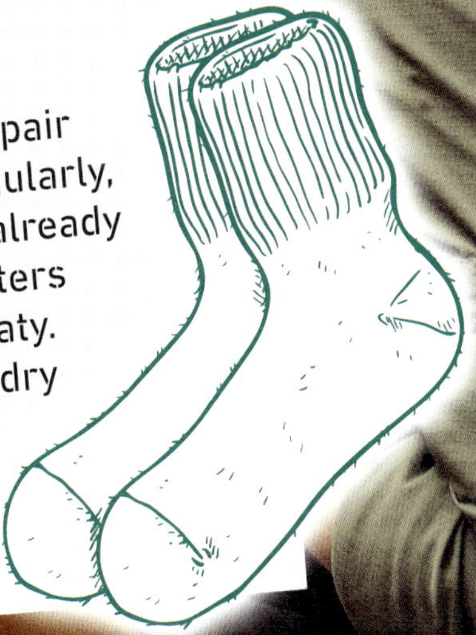

Hikers should always carry a spare pair of socks and change their socks regularly, even if it is into dry ones that have already been worn. Socks help prevent blisters and keep feet from getting too sweaty. By changing sweaty, wet socks for dry ones, feet will feel fresh and dry. Dirty socks should be hung in the Sun to dry at the end of each day.

FIND WATER

Water is more important than food to people lost in the desert. A person can survive about three weeks without food, but only two to three days without water. Finding water is a priority for anyone lost or stranded in the desert.

FOLLOW THE WILDLIFE

Desert wildlife can give clues to help find water in the desert. People should listen for bird sounds and watch the sky for flocks of birds, because birds usually circle over water or head toward it. Insects, such as groups of flies or mosquitoes, are usually found near water. Animal tracks, such as those of the gemsbok, which is found in Africa's Kalahari Desert, can lead to drinking water, especially if they are heading downhill.

gemsbok, Kalahari Desert

FIND HIDDEN RIVERS

Dark-green plants can be a sign of hidden desert **springs** and underground rivers. Hikers can look for a dry streambed, or channel where water used to flow, and follow it to the lowest point. Next to this, they should dig a hole, so water can seep, or slowly leak, from the underground stream into the hole. If possible, before drinking it, they should boil the water to kill any harmful **bacteria**.

A dry streambed can lead to a source of water, but sleeping or camping in a streambed can be dangerous. Sudden rainfall could cause it to flood.

WATER CHAIN

Cacti grow in most deserts except polar and sandy deserts, such as the Sahara. The spines on cacti gather moisture from early morning fog, then the moisture drips down to the roots. Insects drink the plants' juices, and mammals eat the insects. Cacti also have long, shallow roots that can suck up water from the ground after a rain shower. Many cacti contain **toxins** that can make people sick, so they must not drink cactus juice unless they know it is not poisonous.

The pleats in a saguaro straighten out when the plant is filled with water.

BE PREPARED

Desert hikers lost in the northern hemisphere can use a compass to look for the north side of canyons. The north side gets less Sun, so it is more likely to have pockets of rainwater.

SURVIVAL STORY

MILES FROM CIVILIZATION: JOHN F. CAMPBELL

Cowboy and artist, John F. Campbell, was hiking with friends in the mountains of Guadalupe, which rise above the stony Chihuahuan Desert west of Texas, when the group realized it had run out of water. They were far from anywhere and it was nearly noon, when the scorching Sun is at its hottest. Guadalupe National Park contains lush green areas, but John and his group were in the dry, parched, desert areas.

TOO MUCH, TOO FAST

Campbell realized that his team had been taking great gulps of water when they felt thirsty, instead of steady sips regularly. Taking huge gulps is not helpful, since the water is released from the body as sweat. By taking smaller sips, the body is more likely to stay hydrated. Some of the team were already becoming dehydrated, suffering from stomach cramps, headaches, and dizziness. They began the search for water.

NEEDING WATER

As an expert backpacker, Campbell knew that there are several ways to collect water in desertlike **terrain**. People can dig a hole and place a container inside the hole to catch **condensation** as it forms into water droplets. Another option is to tie a clear plastic bag around the leaves of a plant and wait for water to collect. But both these options take time, possibly many hours, and the group needed water right away.

UNDERSTANDING THE DESERT

Campbell decided that the quickest way to get water was to drain the yucca plants growing all around them. Yucca plants survive in dry conditions by storing water in their roots and thick, fleshy leaves. They also have a waxy coating that keeps moisture from **evaporating** in the hot sunshine. However, yucca plant leaves have sharp, pointed ends that cause injury if not handled properly.

Carefully, Campbell used a knife to strip off a few yucca leaves. He squeezed out enough moisture from the leaves so that everyone could have small sips as they set off again in search of their camp. Eventually, the group made it safely back to the camp, thanks to Campbell's survival knowledge and the desert yucca plants.

Yucca plants have sharp, pointed leaves to keep desert animals from eating them.

STAY IN THE SHADE

To prevent dehydration, it is better to travel through a hot desert at night, when it is much cooler. Traveling at night can keep a person's body from losing about 3 quarts (3 l) of water per day. It is best to build shelters and forage, or look, for food in the early mornings and evenings when it is not so hot.

Resting during the day and keeping the head and face covered can help prevent sunstroke.

FIND SUN SHELTER

Many desert animals, such as gerbils, toads, and tortoises, burrow under the sand during the day to keep out of the Sun. The tortoise also has a long tongue that it can use to lick its head and shoulders to keep cool. Other animals find shelter under rocks, small shrubs, or in the shade of cacti. Like desert animals, people should look for shade during the day. They can make a shelter and rest there.

AVOID HOT SAND

During the day, the ground becomes hot from the Sun. Sand, especially, can become very hot, and it will burn. If people sit or lie down on the hot ground, the heat will cause their body to lose more water and speed up dehydration. Desert animals have evolved many different ways to avoid contact with the hot sand. For example, sidewinder snakes move in a special sideways wriggle, so that their body touches the sand for only a few seconds. In Australia, kangaroos scratch away the top sand and lie down on the cooler ground underneath. This helps keep their body temperature down.

HOW TO BUILD A TRENCH SHELTER

A trench shelter can help protect people from the hot Sun during the day and the cold at night. To build a trench shelter, a hole or trench must be dug in the sand. By leaving a gap at one end of the hole or trench, the person will be able to slide into the trench. The trench is then covered by laying branches or sticks over the top. A **tarp** or piece of plastic is put over this and held down with heavy objects, such as rocks.

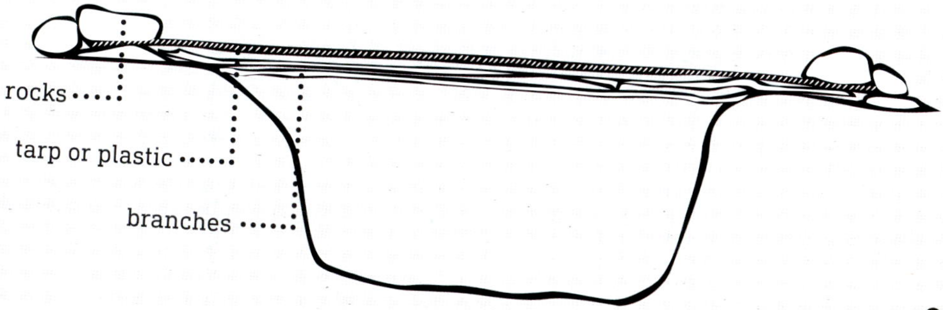

Nights in the desert can be very cold. A fire can be used to keep warm at night, to cook food, to keep away animals, and to use as a signal for help. In the desert, food is not as essential as water. Eating also makes people thirstier, so if water is limited, people should try not to eat.

EATING INSECTS

If food is necessary, insects can be an easy option to catch and cook. Insects that people can eat include locusts, ants, grasshoppers, and crickets. It is better to cook insects before eating them. This is to kill any **parasites** or bacteria the insects may be carrying. Insects can be thread on a thin twig with a sharpened end and then roasted over a fire. It is important to avoid eating hairy caterpillars because they may be poisonous.

Desert beetles are fine to eat, but bright-colored ones could be poisonous.

EATING PLANTS

Many desert plants are poisonous, so only plants that can be identified as harmless should be eaten. Cacti fruit can be eaten, but it is better to lightly roast the fruit over a fire first to remove spines. The young pads on prickly pear cacti can be eaten by preparing them in the same way. Any plants that have a milky sap or red beans must never be eaten.

prickly pear plant, Sonoran Desert

HOW TO MAKE A FIRE IN THE DESERT

Before survivors make a fire, they need to choose the right spot. An area sheltered from the wind will mean fewer drafts and less risk of the fire jumping. To make a fire, dig a small pit, and put rocks around it to contain the fire. Dry twigs and branches can be put in the pit. A fire needs tinder to get it started. Tinder is any kind of dry material that will ignite well. This could be leaves and grasses. Most emergency packs contain fire-starting material, which can be used to light a fire. Next, kindling, such as dry twigs and branches, is added to get the fire going. It is important to keep kindling next to a fire to feed it if it starts to burn down.

SURVIVAL STORY

THE ROAR OF LIONS: KALAHARI PLANE CRASH

In 2000, a light aircraft crashed in the Kalahari, a hot desert in Botswana, southern Africa. Just before the crash, the pilot, Costa Markanadatos, reported an oil leak in the plane and decided to make an emergency landing. The pilot tried to land the plane in a clearing, but one of the wings caught a tree, and the plane burst into flames.

SURVIVING THE CRASH

Costa and the four passengers survived the crash. However, they were off course so could not be sure that a rescue helicopter would find them. They knew they needed to get help if they were to survive the desert. The passengers and Costa drew straws to see who would look for help. Costa and one of the passengers, Carl du Plessis, were chosen, and so they set out in scorching temperatures. Meanwhile, the others sheltered from the Sun under a small group of trees.

FOLLOWING THE TRAIL OF ELEPHANTS

The Kalahari has herds of elephants. Costa and Carl decided to follow an elephant trail, so that they would not be wandering around in circles. They had taken a small bag of food that they had **salvaged** from the plane, and they drank water that collected in puddles after a heavy downpour of rain. To escape the heat, Costa and Carl bathed in the muddy water at **watering holes** used by elephants. The men had no **navigation equipment** so had to use the Sun to find their way.

LIVING IN FEAR

Costa and Carl lived in fear that they would come across a herd of elephants, but luckily, they never did. At night, they could hear the roar of lions in the distance but never saw any. During their journey, they both suffered badly from blisters and mosquito bites. Eventually, after four days, they found a desert lodge and radioed for help. They had walked more than 124 miles (200 km). They gave the details of the position of the plane wreck, so the other passengers could be found and rescued.

RESCUE

Meanwhile, the passengers at the plane wreck had been desperately trying to stay positive about being rescued, but with every day that passed, rescue seemed less likely. They could hardly believe it when they saw aircraft finally coming for them. They were suffering from minor burns, back injuries, and dehydration, but amazingly, all of the passengers and the pilot made a full recovery.

Elephants cover themselves in mud as protection from the heat of the Sun. Humans in the desert can use a similar technique to protect themselves.

KEEP WARM AT NIGHT

When the cold sets in at night, it is important to avoid hypothermia, this is when heat is lost and body temperature drops dangerously low. Signs of hypothermia include shivering, dropping things, and feeling confused. At night, wearing thin layers of clothing will keep the air circulating around the body. The air **insulates** the body and keeps people warmer.

STAY DRY

Hypothermia can also happen when people lose body heat as their clothes cool on their skin. Clothing absorbs sweat during the day, and at night, moisture from the damp clothing evaporates. The moisture carries body heat away from the body, so people are more likely to get colder faster. Drying off sweat and changing clothing at **twilight** will help prevent evaporation at night.

Wearing a hat at night can help keep too much heat from leaving a person's body.

UNDERGROUND AT NIGHT

Most desert animals have adapted so that they are nocturnal. This means that they sleep during the day when it is hot and come out at night when it is cooler. Reptiles are **cold-blooded** animals. They need the Sun to warm them, so they sleep underground during the night and come out in daylight to lie in the Sun.

collared lizard, Sonoran Desert

BE PREPARED

In a hot desert, it is always best to travel at night and rest during the day. But if this is not possible, making camp next to large rocks will help you keep warm. The rocks will store some of the day's heat and act as heaters. Sleeping off of the ground will prevent the body from losing more heat through the cold ground. Building a bed of twigs and leaves, or placing clothing or a sleeping bag on the ground, will provide a warmer barrier.

BEWARE STINGS AND BITES

When making camp, preparing a fire, or doing other tasks, always check carefully that animals, such as scorpions, snakes, and spiders, are not sheltering under stones, in leaves and twigs, or in rotting wood. Hands and feet should be kept safe, too. When climbing over rocks, logs, or boulders, people must be careful where they step.

BEASTLY BUGS

Bugs are a vital part of the hot desert food supply, providing food and moisture for a wide range of animals. However, some can cause nasty rashes and itching, and can pass on diseases. Protecting the body by keeping as much skin covered as possible, especially ankles and hands, is important. Covering bare skin in mud can help keep bugs away because they cannot bite through mud.

desert bug, Atacama Desert

BE PREPARED

In the morning, shoes and clothing must be checked to make sure scorpions and insects have not crawled into them during the night. The simplest way to do this is to shake the clothing and shoes.

scorpion

LEAVE SNAKES ALONE

Snakes will bite if they are disturbed or threatened. It is best to leave snakes alone and keep at least 10 feet (3 m) away. If someone is bitten by a **venomous** snake, the bite needs to be treated immediately. If possible, the bitten area should be kept at or below heart level to slow down the venom spreading through the body. A **splint** to keep the bite area as still as possible can be made. Keeping still can also help slow the venom spread until the person can get to the hospital.

Snakes **hibernate** in winter and are most active during the day in spring and fall, and in the cool evenings of summer. Rattlesnakes have a triangular-shaped head, a thick body, and a rattle on the tail. Each desert **biome** has different kinds of rattlesnakes. Diamondback, sidewinders, and tiger rattlesnakes are just some of those that live in the Sonoran Desert. The western diamondback is common in the Mojave Desert in California.

People climbing on rocks must be careful of any holes where snakes or scorpions might be resting.

SICK AND ALONE: VICTORIA GROVER

In 2012, Victoria Grover drove into the Utah desert to go on a hike. She left her car by a trail and set out. Enjoying the wide-open space and freedom of the desert, she did not realize how late it was getting or how far away from her car she had walked.

CAMPING FOR THE NIGHT

Victoria started to make her way back to the car because it was getting dark. When she slipped near a cliff edge, she decided to stay put for the night and get back to her car when it was light. There was plenty of wood around, so she made a fire to keep herself warm and keep the coyotes away. The next morning, she started her journey back to the car. As she was jumping down a series of rocky ledges, she slipped and broke her lower left leg in several places.

For many people, a hike in the desert can seem like a fun sport. However, it is important to remember that the desert is a very dangerous biome.

LOST AND INJURED

When she had set out on her hike the day before, for safety, Victoria had given her route to a staff member at the hotel where she was staying. But this person left for vacation without informing anyone else that Victoria was out hiking. Now she was lost and injured in a place called Box-Death Hollow Wilderness. She didn't know if anyone was searching for her. Victoria had no food, and her broken leg made it too painful for her to walk or stand. She had to move around by shuffling along on her bottom.

In pain and with a lot of effort, Victoria made her way to the edge of a stream so that she was close to water. Victoria had done a desert survival course a few years earlier and remembered some of the advice she had learned. She used a branch to make a splint for her injured leg, tying the splint in place with her scarf.

DAY AND NIGHT

Victoria rested and slept during the day. She was unable to gather firewood to make a fire at night and had only a poncho to shelter her from the Sun, cold, and wind. At night, she wrapped her head and face in her poncho, to capture warmth from her breath.

The next night, it rained heavily. Victoria was now hungry, tired, and soaked through. On the sixth day, a helicopter flew overhead. Victoria waved frantically to attract the pilot's attention, and fortunately, that worked. Victoria was safely airlifted to the hospital and made a full recovery. She was lucky to have survived.

Deserts are tough places. The extreme temperatures, lack of easy access to water, and remote location mean a desert adventure could turn dangerous if explorers are not prepared. If lost in a desert, it is best to keep calm and assess the situation. The survival skills highlighted in this book can help.

KEEP CLOSE, KEEP TOGETHER

It is rare, but sometimes airplanes crash or vehicles break down in the desert. Experts say that the keys to keeping alive and safe are staying with the plane or car and waiting for rescue, and remaining together as a group. People must not panic but rather assess the situation and make a plan.

MARK A TRAIL

Sometimes, it is necessary to search for food and water, but this should never be done without leaving a trail to follow back. Rocks and twigs can be placed in the shape of an arrow so rescuers can follow the trail. Sweating as little as possible can help prevent dehydration, so people should rest every 10 minutes.

HOW TO SEND A DISTRESS SIGNAL

The standard international distress signal is three of anything, such as three blasts of noise from a car horn or whistle. Sound carries best at twilight, just before it gets dark. Three large piles of rocks placed in a triangle also signals distress. If building a fire, making it smoky by adding a layer of green leaves will help rescuers find those who are lost. Those with a vehicle could burn a tire to make thick, black smoke. Anything shiny, such as aluminum foil or a mirror, can be used to flash signals at rescue planes or cars and people in the distance.

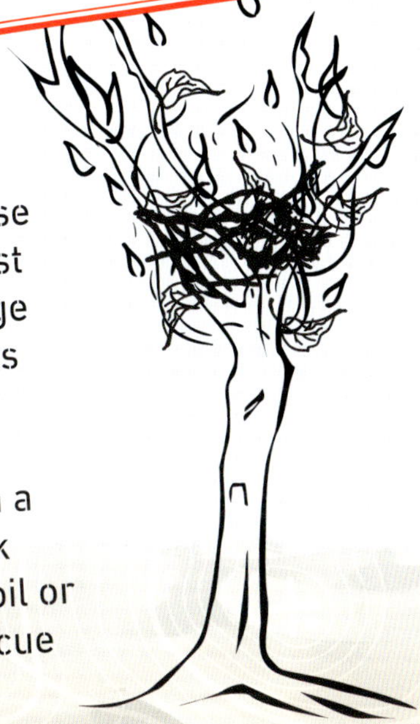

A broken-down car or an airplane can provide shelter during the cold desert night.

GLOSSARY

adapted Developed skills or physical features over time to help animals live in a certain biome

bacteria Single-celled organisms that are invisible to the human eye

biome A large area where plants and animals naturally live. A biome is also recognized by other features, such as how much water it has and what its weather is like.

cold-blooded Describes animals that cannot control their own body heat

condensation The process of water vapor in the air cooling and turning into water

dehydration Excessive loss of water from a person's body

dune A hill of sand created by wind

evaporating When liquid is changing into a gas and becoming part of the air

flare A light that shines brightly for a short time; used in emergencies

hibernate To go into a sleep in the winter, where the body slows down and feeds on its own fat

insulates Protects against something, such as cold

navigation equipment Devices that people use to find their way from one place to another, such as a map or a compass

nomadic Describes people who move from one place to another

parasites Organisms that live and feed on other animals

priority The order in which things are important

purifying Removing harmful substances

salvaged Saved

sandstorms Strong winds that blow large amounts of sand in a certain direction

splint A hard object, such as a piece of wood, that holds a broken bone in place

springs Places where underground water comes to the surface

stable Fixed or steady

sunstroke Illness caused by being in the hot sunshine for too long

tarp A large waterproof piece of cloth or plastic that is rainproof and used as a covering

terrain The physical features of an area of land

toxins Poisonous substances found in some living things

twilight The time just before night when the sky is getting darker and the Sun has set, but it is not completely dark

venomous Capable of injecting poison through a bite

watering holes Places where animals gather to drink

LEARNING MORE

Find out more about deserts and how to survive them.

Aloian, Molly. *The Sahara Desert* (Deserts Around the World). Crabtree Publishing Company, 2012.

Grylls, Bear. *Bear Grylls Survival Skills: Desert*. Bear Grylls Publishing, 2018.

Martin, Claudia. *Make It Out Alive in a Desert* (Makerspace Survival). PowerKids Press, 2017.

Towell, Colin. *Survival for Beginners: A Step-by-Step Guide to Camping and Outdoor Skills*. DK Children, 2019.

WEBSITES

Check out more ways that people can survive if stranded in the desert:
www.desertusa.com/desert-activity/desert-survival-skills.html

Discover how animals survive in the desert:
www.nationalgeographic.com/animals/2019/04/extreme-animals-that-live-in-deserts

Learn more about the desert biome at:
www.nationalgeographic.com/environment/habitats/deserts

Find out how different nomadic tribes live in the desert at:
https://theculturetrip.com/africa/articles/10-nomadic-communities-and-their-fascinating-lives

INDEX AND ABOUT THE AUTHOR

INDEX

ABOUT THE AUTHOR

Sarah Eason has written a lot of books about biomes and the animals that live in them and have adapted to survive there. On her travels, she has also visited different biomes, including oceans, grasslands, forests, and mountains. If she journeys to a desert one day, she will make sure that the useful information and advice in this book travels with her!